Daily Confessions For

IMPACTING YOUR WORLD

Transforming Destinies with the Bread of Life

GODKULTURE
PUBLISHING

Daily Confessions For

IMPACTING YOUR WORLD

Transforming Destinies with the Bread of Life

J. E Bamidele Sturdivant

Unless otherwise indicated, all Scripture quotations in this book are from the New King James Version of the Bible.

Daily Confessions For Impacting Your World

Copyright © 2011 by **J.E Bamidele Sturdivant**

ISBN: 978-0-9839613-1-4

Library of Congress Control Number: 2012940055

Published by
GodKulture Publishing
Chicago, Illinois

Phone: 815-630-9890
Email: publishing@Godkulture.org
www.GodKulturepublishing.com

This publication may not be reproduced, stored in a retrieval system, or transmitted in whole or in part, in any form or by any means, elec-tronic, mechanical, photocopying, recording, or otherwise, without prior written permission of the publisher.

All rights reserved.

Printed in United States of America

DEDICATION

This book is dedicated to the memory, ministry and example of those great "Fathers Of The Faith", who laid the foundation of a consistent walk of holiness and a confident confession.

I further recognize the modern day "Generals" whose steadfast obedience in *this* compromised generation, shines a ray of hope for a people who have lost their way.

May the Almighty God fulfill His promise to your *seed*!

ACKNOWLEDGMENTS

I wish to acknowledge and thank God for Nigeria's prophet (and my Daddy) E.A. Adeboye, and my Mummy, Foluke Adeboye.

> *...As your days are, so may your strength be!*
> **(Deuteronomy 33:25b)**

I thank the Almighty for every RCCG parish worldwide.
May He send you help from the sanctuary!
(Psalm 20:2a)

For my family, ministry and 'spiritual' children, may you forever "live" in the *"over flow"*! **(Psalm 23:5)**

To my wife, Pamela ("Modupe"), may the Almighty God *"...Grant you according to your heart's desire"* **(Psalm 20:4a)**. God bless you for your steadfast love!

TABLE OF CONTENTS

Preface 3

Introduction 5

Confession 1: Setting The Order 9

Confession 2: Boundless Possibilities 11

Confession 3: Instrument Of Change 13

Confession 4: Developing Godly Relationships 15

Confession 5: Ungodly Conformity 17

Confession 6: Self Discovery 19

Confession 7: Taking Charge 21

Confession 8: Dominion Lifestyle 23

Confession 9: The Power Of Words 25

Confession 10: Consistency 27

Confession 11: Making A Positive Confession 29

Confession 12: The God In You 31

Confession 13: My Position In Christ 33

Confession 14: Divine Confidence 35

Confession 15: Growing Faith 37

Confession 16: Use The Keys 39

Confession 17: Hang On 41

Confession 18: The Final Authority 43

Confession 19: Start Planting 45

Confession 20: A Little Daily 47

Confession 21: Inside Out 49

Confession 22: Walk In The Light 51

Confession 23: Holiness Is A Lifestyle 53

Confession 24: Living A Life Of Love 55

Confession 25: The Rock Of Our Salvation 57

Confession 26: Waiting On The Lord 59

Confession 27: Purity of Heart 61

Confession 28: Faith And Holiness 63

Confession 29: The Clothing Of Power 65

Confession 30: Press In! 67

Confession 31: Daily Dependence On God 69

Confession 32: The Sanctified Life 71

Confession 33: Christ: The Way Of Life 73

Confession 34: A Vessel Unto Honor 75

Confession 35: Equipped To Win 77

Confession 36: Ministering From The Overflow 79

Confession 37: Speak Like God 81

Confession 38: Doing The Works Of Jesus 83

Confession 39: Occupy Until Jesus Comes 85

Confession 40: The World Is Waiting For You 87

Meditative Prayer 89

PREFACE

Even so the tongue is a little member and boasts great things. See how great a forest a little fire kindles!

(James 3:5)

In this simple passage of scripture, James lifts for us that, what causes many to do or not do; accomplish great things or nothing at all; be at peace with themselves or live a life of misery and regret..."rest" in the power of their tongue. Meaning, *the words that one speaks!*

The mistake that many make, in regard to conversations, expressing themselves, arguments or discussions, is that, they underestimate the power and potency of the tongue's *(words)* influence, because of its size *(...a little member...)*. However, it has the ability to change or turn the course of an individual's *day, desire* or even their *destiny* by the words that come out of their mouth.

Look also at ships: Although they are so large and are driven by fierce winds, they are turned by a very small rudder wherever the pilot desires.

(James 3:4)

What you plan to do or be; where you plan to go or hope to accomplish can be either **pushed into possibility** or **aborted before its attempted**... simply by the power of your speech! You will either *affirm* what God has spoken over your life or *assassinate* what was supposed to happen by the words that you speak!

*...whoever **says**....and does not doubt...but believes that those things he **says** will be done, he will have whatever he **says**.*

(Mark 11:23)

Your words are 'self-fulfilling' prophecies that "create" pictures and scenarios that *go into* one's future and cause to *materialize* what has been *verbalized!*

Remember *this*, Beloved...

- ➢ **We are *created* in the image of God**

    So God created man in His own image;...

    (Genesis 1:27)

- ➢ **Whatever God wanted to *see*, He *said***

    *Then God **said**, let there be light;...and God **saw** the light...*

    (Genesis 1:3, 4)

- ➢ **He *gave* that same authority to Adam**

    *...The Lord God formed every beast...and brought them to Adam to see what he would call them. And **whatever Adam called** each living creature, **that was its name.***

    (Genesis 2:19)

Like God, *your words create your world.* Whatever He declared out of His mouth, He saw it with His eyes. This book, *Daily Confessions For Impacting Your World*, gives practical steps on how you can transform both your life *and* your desired goals through the power of your confession.

The more of His Word that you have in your heart, the more of His Word that will come out of your mouth.

...For out of the abundance of the heart the mouth speaks.

(Matthew 12:34)

You *can* change your *world* with your *words!*

J.E Bamidele Sturdivant

INTRODUCTION

It is imperative that *everyone* who names the name of Jesus Christ, *live* by the words that are declared in the Holy Scriptures. We can get the results that God got by saying what He says in His Word. God leaves the naming of our environmental state up to the words we speak concerning it (Genesis 2:19).

So then, if it is the *same* word, and its power is not related to only inanimate objects, then it stands to reason that the power of confession *must* work when one is dealing with oneself. We *do* have the ability to speak over our lives and make a *proclamation* concerning a *situation*.

But **the word is very near you**, *in your mouth and in your heart*, **that you may do it**.
(Deuteronomy 30:14)

This being true, how can we talk ourselves out of our troubles? The problem in much of Christendom is that since so many have had such traumatic backgrounds, they are *fearful* to operate by *faith*, and are *still* blaming someone else for their pain or have *settled* for mediocrity and refuse to try.

Hence, they spiritualize their stagnation and claim to be "waiting on the Lord" or being taught patience, when the *truth* of the matter is, they have deceived themselves into putting *all* the activity on God's part and relinquishing themselves from having to *do* anything. So, when nothing happens (again), they can have someone (God) or something (life) to blame for them *still* being in the same place.

Thus, the need for a *confession*! Why? It requires the confessor to become *pro-active* in the producing of results. It *must* be personal! How then can we access the *power of confession* that is in us when it comes to our problems? What makes authority even more effective and life impacting for the believer is knowing *Who* has given us the authority that we are to utilize! Now, some would say, "that was only for the disciples," but look at this…

*But **you** shall receive power when the Holy Spirit has come upon **you**…*
(Acts 1:8)

Clearly this scripture bears out the fact that both power and authority have been delegated to each believer to impact their world for the good and the glory of God's Kingdom. Yet, any authority is *only* as good as the One who *gives* it.

In that case, what validates the authenticity and credibility of what's been given to us to use is the integrity and command of the One who possesses it. Why then are so many believers overwhelmed and constantly thrown around or taken aback every time some new situation or circumstance arises? It is because of what they allow their lips to utter in the face of the challenges that confront them.

Many of us have not prepared our hearts or our mouths for an affirmative (positive) confession to adversity *prior* to coming under attack! Consequently, when we are in the midst of a dilemma, we respond based on our unpreparedness, the upheaval in our emotions or the disorder in our surroundings. Responding this way has been our 'practice' for so long until it is what has become natural or *the norm* to us!

The whole creation has been groaning together in the pains of labor until now, because the children of God are not exhibiting their divine prowess. Believers all over the world are looking elsewhere for the next move of the Holy Spirit, but in reality they need to let go of their flimsy excuses and come to a place of rest in God. Actually, the next move of God is neither here nor there but *in* us, because we are all created in the image of God and have His nature. We need to set time aside to activate this divine nature in us so that we can be a blessing to our world.

This book reveals how to become a vessel of honor in the hands of God. Understanding certain principles and putting them into practice will enable us to attain greater heights in Him. There is a meditative prayer on pages 89, 90 derived from a number of scriptures. The referenced scriptures are stated on the following page for your in-depth study of them. Meditating and praying them daily will produce great results in your walk with God.

We need to be good stewards of His manifold grace in our lives, because the world is waiting for *our* manifestation (Romans 8:19-22). We have been crucified with Christ, therefore, Jesus lives in us and works through us since we are His branches. As a result of this, whatever we say with our mouth will come to pass, but the choice is ours to live like Him, because…

We *can* **only** *do all things through Christ who strengthens* **us**.
(Philippians 4:13, Paraphrased)

Confession 1

SETTING THE ORDER

By faith we understand that the worlds were framed by the word of God, so that the things which are seen were not made of things which are visible.
(Hebrews 11:3)

Daily Word Weapon: Genesis 1:1-4;
Matthew 12:33, 34; I Corinthians 14:40

In the beginning, God created our planet with a guidance system built into the very elements of the earth, the north and south magnetic poles. When humankind made this astonishing discovery, it opened the entire world to be navigated. Likewise at the beginning of creation, when the world was in disarray, the Holy Spirit of God came as a spiritual force into the world to create order out of chaos. It was the Spirit of God that breathed upon men of old to pen the Scripture.

These two, the Spirit and the written Word, worked together within us to provide a spiritual directional system for our life. God's speaking brought order, shape and light. Likewise, in our world, when we make this amazing finding, God's spiritual world will be opened to us to chart a new course. By speaking God's Word over our situations, we limit the control that the enemy can have over our world and us.

The journey to this divine order starts when we allow God's Words to saturate us, so that it can influence our thoughts and ultimately our heart. Out of the overflow of God's Word in our heart, our mouth speaks. Automatically, our decisions follow what we speak.

After making decisions out of what we speak, our actions over an extensive period of time become our habit. In so doing, our lives begin to line up with the eternal truth of God's Word.

Impacting My World Confession

I declare that from today onward, my world will line up with God's Word. I am disciplined and my environment is subject to God's will for my life. My priorities agree with the destiny that God has for me and I am no longer moved by my emotional instability or indecisive stagnation. In Jesus' Name, I Declare It! Amen.

What is the Spirit saying to me?

_____
_____
_____
_____
_____
_____
_____
_____
_____
_____

He who has an ear, let him hear what the Spirit says...
(Revelation 2:11)

Confession 2

BOUNDLESS POSSIBILITIES

In the beginning was the Word, and the Word was with God, and the Word was God. ²He was in the beginning with God. ³All things were made through Him, and without Him nothing was made that was made.
(John 1:1-3)

Daily Word Weapon: Mark 9:21-24;
Ephesians 3:20; Philippians 2:5-11

Many people have made frantic efforts to make progress in their respective endeavors, but all their striving proved to no avail. Such people might think that it is very difficult to experience limitless opportunities. The question is: Is there such a thing as a world of no limits? There is a place in God where one lives and enjoys a world of no limits. It is a world where one operates the way one wants at all times in accordance to God's Word.

Think about it... By God's Word, planets and all their inhabitants, all their inventions, all their knowledge, etc. were spoken into existence! Meaning, beyond what our technology has discovered, there are people whose life and achievements we know nothing about.

The book of Genesis states that there was a time when God told Abraham to lift up his eyes and look towards the north, south, east and west, that as far as his eyes could see would be given to him (Genesis 13:14, 15). Abraham believed God's Word, and he entered into a world of boundless possibilities. With God all things are possible.

The problem is that there are some who don't *believe* that. It is when we believe what God says, that we move from the realm of natural to spiritual. In that spirit realm, we gain access to revelation, which activates our divine nature to lay hold of our inheritance. If we are not empowered by the Word, we will not attain to our full potential in Christ Jesus. We need this power of God's Word, if we hope to obtain a world of no limits.

Impacting My World Confession

I refuse to limit myself to my past mistakes and pains or my ancestry past. I confess that God's Word has given me limitless potential and opportunity to live better than I can ever imagine. I denounce my closed minded way of thinking and embrace the mind of Christ for my life. In Jesus' Name, I Declare It! Amen.

What is the Spirit saying to me?

_____
_____
_____
_____
_____
_____
_____
_____
_____

He who has an ear, let him hear what the Spirit says...
(Revelation 2:11)

Confession 3

INSTRUMENT OF CHANGE

While we do not look at the things which are seen, but at the things which are not seen. For the things which are seen are temporary, but the things which are not seen are eternal.
(I Corinthians 4:18)

Daily Word Weapon: Psalm 119:89; Matthew 24:35; II Corinthians 1:20

Many give up on the promise or prophecy spoken over their lives because of their current circumstances that seem unfavorable. However, God specializes in calling light out of darkness to demonstrate His power and to bring Himself glory. It is our responsibility to meditate on such promises until they come to pass. God's Word, which is able make the impossible possible, is readily made available to us. It is like a refreshing rain that waters seeds of prophecy in order to bring them to fruition.

God's Word never changes and it does not fail under any circumstance. It does not matter what is happening all around you, God's Word remains constant. Every Word of God is flawless and you can always rely on it. You can rest upon it forever and the *old* truth of His Word is ever *new*.

When we know God's Word, it keeps our spiritual walk from slipping and it satisfies the hunger of our souls. It is also sufficient for the wise and it is a key weapon to face temptations and trials. The Word of God is a healer, comfort and strength. You can draw strength from it at any time, even when other things fail.

Do you doubt how some prophecies will come to pass in your life? Why not search the scriptures concerning that topic and meditate on it day and night. When you confess His Word with faith and boldness, you are saying exactly what God has said. As a result, He will agree with you, your contrary situation will line up with His Word, and your prophecies will become realities.

Impacting My World Confession

I confess that my circumstances are under the control of God's Word. Nothing is too hard for Him! Although I may have some situations that are not favorable, I confess that the favor of God rests upon my life. What He says concerning me is what I abide by. In Jesus' Name, I Declare It! Amen.

What is the Spirit saying to me?

_____
_____
_____
_____
_____
_____
_____
_____
_____

He who has an ear, let him hear what the Spirit says...
(Revelation 2:11)

Confession 4

DEVELOPING GODLY RELATIONSHIPS

Then he went and joined himself to a citizen of that country, and he sent him into his fields to feed swine.
(Luke 15:15)

Daily Word Weapon: I Samuel 30:6;
I Corinthians 15:33; II Corinthians 6:14-18

Knowing how to choose friends is one of the most important skills you'll ever develop. Friends are something we all want; people we can trust, who we can share with, who can help us and we can help in return. No doubt we all wish for such friends. Of course, some can be trusted more than others. There are some we can enjoy socializing with but we would not share our inner feelings with. There are grades and categories of friendships. We need all sorts of friends, but we need close friends.

There is no doubt about the fact that Jesus is the best friend we can have. He can always be trusted and never lets us down or hurts us. Nevertheless, we still need those individuals who can interact with us the way Jesus does. Likewise, people also need us as a close friend as well.

To be a friend like Jesus, we can't just talk about being a close friend. We need something more than that. We need the Lord himself in the relationship. This can be called a *godly friend*. A godly friend is going to be like Jesus to us and we are going to be like Jesus to them.

Destinies of countless thousands of people have been destroyed because of bad relationships. Many of the trouble places that we find ourselves in are a direct result of who we have *tied* our self into. It is a whole lot easier *not* to get into a dilemma than it is to get out of it, once you are in. Watch yourself!

We need the type of friends who can encourage and challenge us in line with God's Word and sharpen us spiritually. Any other kind will *dull our cutting edge* as we journey to our destiny.

Impacting My World Confession

I am in a new season of my life. Toxic people, attitudes and situations can no longer be connected with me! I understand that *this* can be lonely. I may have to re-learn myself. But in the end...I *will* have peace. In Jesus' Name, I Declare It! Amen.

What is the Spirit saying to me?

_____
_____
_____
_____
_____
_____
_____
_____
_____

He who has an ear, let him hear what the Spirit says...
(Revelation 2:11)

Confession 5

UNGODLY CONFORMITY

And he would gladly have filled his stomach with the pods that the swine ate, and no one gave him anything.
(Luke 15:16)

Daily Word Weapon: Psalm 118:17; Romans 12:1, 2; II Timothy 3:12-17

The challenges of life can come out of our negligence to a command of God, a test He is giving, or (without notice), as an attack from the enemy. But we should not allow it to stop us from moving in God's will for us. The enemy will try very hard to discourage us from worshiping God with all of our passion because, he knows that a believer on fire for God will move mountains. Paul described himself as an 'ambassador in chains' in his letter to the Church in Ephesus. Even though he was locked away in a prison, he adamantly refused to allow his circumstances to dictate or alter his identity.

You may be *in chains* right now, but you remain the Lord's ambassador because you have been washed by the blood of the Lamb. Can you imagine Paul chained up in that dungeon, throwing up his hands saying, "That's it. It's over. I am finished!?" Instead the apostle emboldened himself as an ambassador of Jesus Christ, not intimidated or ashamed, because he was not chained in his Spirit, he was only bound in the flesh. Remember what he included in his letter to the Church at Philippi, *"I can do all things through Christ who strengthens me."*

Whenever you are in the pit of trouble, hopelessness could settle in and make you comfortable. Do not allow yourself to be defined by your past, or chained by your current circumstances. Speak aloud to the contrary situation and it will fade away. Remember I John 4:4, "...*He who is in you is greater than he who is in the world.*"

Impacting My World Confession

I refuse to allow my identity to ever be determined by my circumstance, be it past or present. I am defined by my destiny in Christ Jesus and not the dilemma I am currently in or going through. Therefore, I declare that I am a winner, even it looks otherwise. In Jesus' Name, I Declare It! Amen.

What is the Spirit saying to me?

_____
_____
_____
_____
_____
_____
_____
_____
_____
_____

He who has an ear, let him hear what the Spirit says...
(Revelation 2:11)

Confession 6

SELF DISCOVERY

*But when **he came to himself**, he said, 'How many of my father's hired servants have bread enough and to spare, and I perish with hunger!*
(Luke 15:17)

Daily Word Weapon: Genesis 1:26, 27; Psalm 8; Psalm 139:14

Self discovery is the *process of getting in touch with your true self*, though it is not usually as straightforward as we might like. To *be* yourself, and be at peace *with* yourself, you must truly *know* yourself. The reason for this is because the *real* you, the spirit man, get's "hidden" within the soulish realm of your makeup. Our ego has a way of disguising our true self, so it requires some effort to unveil it.

We discover our real self when our ego has been stripped. The prodigal son in Luke 15:11-32 derived his self esteem in the amount of riches in his possession. *He only came to himself* when he started to be in want, after he had squandered everything that his father gave him. He had never *been* himself, though he had everything *to* himself.

In the same way, many people today live by the opinions of others concerning themselves. It is necessary that we have a positive outlook of ourselves. We cannot afford to live or die by the estimation that others have of us. This reckless son understood clearly how far away he had gone from his place of purpose. However, it took time and adversity to cause him to travel back to his desired haven. That was a great struggle for him.

No matter how far away we are from the process of self discovery, we must make haste to return back to our Maker. Why? Because *in Him we live and move and have our being* (Acts 17:28). God created us uniquely and wonderfully, and it is by returning to Him that we discover our real self. Present yourself to Him daily by renewing your mind with His Word. Then gradually, His perfect will for your life will unfold to you.

Impacting My World Confession

I have not always valued *me* for the unique individual that I am. Mistakes, missteps and poor choices have played down my ability to be confident. Why can I say this? Because I now have a revelation of myself. The *best* me has been waiting for this moment in my life. And you know what? I am ready now! In Jesus' Name, I Declare It! Amen.

What is the Spirit saying to me?

_____
_____
_____
_____
_____
_____
_____
_____
_____

He who has an ear, let him hear what the Spirit says...
(Revelation 2:11)

Confession 7

TAKING CHARGE

Then the LORD God took the man and put him in the garden of Eden to tend and keep it.
(Genesis 2:15)

Daily Word Weapon: Genesis 2:5; Psalm 8:6; I Corinthians 10:13

Despite the fact that God desires to use men on earth to accomplish His divine purposes, He is never in haste to force any man into spiritual leadership. He takes His time to prepare every vessel before He entrusts into his hand a major responsibility. Even if there is a space to be occupied, He might permit it to be so until He finds someone whom He has adequately equipped to pour Himself into. Not even our zeal can make Him accelerate the process of training.

It is a serious concern that many who have not been *formed* by the hand of the Almighty are now *assuming* positions of authority in the church. For instance, John the Baptist was born with a prophecy that he would prepare the way for the Lord Jesus Christ (Luke 1:11-17). Yet, God took him to the wilderness to prepare him for ministry before He revealed him to the nation of Israel. When God calls a man, He also creates a place for him, in which he will be most effective, to operate.

It is when God subjects a vessel to training that the need for enlargement of capacity in grace is perfected. Did you notice that man was formed outside of Eden, and then was put in a place that God had designed with man's strengths in mind? So it is with each of us, He prepares us for what He is about to put us in.

Although we are not in control of how God prepares us, we can be assured and insure the successful progression of our lives by meditating on His Word day and night, and acting on it. In so doing, we will excel because we are cooperating with Him.

Impacting My World Confession

I confess that *I am not overwhelmed, at the end of my rope, under the circumstances,* and *no one has gotten on my last nerve.* What I *am* is in a place that will bring out in me the skills that I did not know I had. I *agree* with God's assessment of me. If I am *in* it, He believes I can handle it and so do I. In Jesus' Name, I Declare It! Amen.

What is the Spirit saying to me?

_____
_____
_____
_____
_____
_____
_____
_____
_____
_____

He who has an ear, let him hear what the Spirit says...
(Revelation 2:11)

Confession 8

DOMINION LIFESTYLE

Out of the ground the LORD God formed every beast of the field and every bird of the air, and brought them to Adam to see what he would call them.
(Genesis 2:19a)

Daily Word Weapon: Deuteronomy 28:12-14; Isaiah 54:17; Ephesians 2:5, 6

Nothing brings more heartache to the Almighty God, than to see his children tormented by the troubles of this world (Luke 12:32). Many are only surviving in life, struggling with distress, sickness and poverty. Why should the princes of the King of kings sit in low places and walk as mere servants on earth? This is a great error! Several christians today *claim they live in power*, but actually, very few *walk in victory*.

In the Garden of Eden, Adam and Eve enjoyed a blessed and prosperous life over which they had dominion. However, after they lost the dominion and authority, they began to experience a hard life. It is not different with us today. Without authority invested in us by God, it is impossible to experience a blessed life. This is why when the Father made us *sons*, He gave us authority.

Not only did He redeem us, He also gave us the right to rule on earth. When you know how to walk in dominion, you will live a life of power and fulfillment. You will *not* be dominated by curses. Our mistrust of others causes us to never fully embrace the idea that God sincerely wants us to be, not only successful, but also to operate in the fullness of our ability. Our skepticism and deceitfulness causes many of us to block our own progress. Why?

We will not allow ourselves to move past our normal sight and see that what God is bringing to us is not to *maim* us, but for us to *name* it. We need to know who we are in Christ Jesus and the authority we have as a believer. This can be attained by meditating and confessing aloud the scriptures that are based on our position in Christ Jesus. A few of them are: Romans 1:6; Romans 3:24; Ephesians 2:5-6; Colossians 3:1, 3.

Impacting My World Confession

No longer will I allow my own insecurities, fears, rejection and past baggage keep me from being open to what God brings my way. I know that by doing this, I will appear vulnerable and may get hurt. However, my faith in God causes me to believe that when the smoke clears and the dust settles, I will still be standing because I am more than a conqueror through Christ who loves me. In Jesus' Name, I Declare It! Amen.

What is the Spirit saying to me?

_____
_____
_____
_____
_____
_____
_____
_____
_____
_____

He who has an ear, let him hear what the Spirit says...
(Revelation 2:11)

Confession 9

THE POWER OF WORDS

...And whatever Adam called each living creature, that was its name.
(Genesis 2: 19b)

Daily Word Weapon: Matthew 12:34;
Romans 4:17, 18; II Corinthians 4:13

Confessing God's Word is not a way to get our own will accomplished but rather, the will of God. As we believe and confess His Word, we are setting ourselves in agreement with God for His plan to come to pass in our lives. A lot of what we have been blaming the devil for and being mad about, is actually the creation of our own mouths. Our idle talk and moody conversation over situations that caught us off guard, has created valleys of depression and killed many of our hopes and dreams.

It would be better and healthier for us if we simply shut up, when we are not sure if it's God or not. Satan wants us to concentrate on our problems so intently, until we get to the point that we assume that the whole thing is hopeless and that no one, not even God, can get us out of our pandemonium. When we are faced with setbacks, it is really important to make a decision not to focus on our problem (as hard as that may be). Instead, it is beneficial to focus on God and begin to speak His Word.

When we focus on His Word, we realize that with Him all things are possible. If we start speaking words in line with His Word, it gets His attention. It does not really matter if none of those things we say are presently a reality in our lives. It is *our* responsibility to start putting on our new nature, which is created in God's image, and start watching our situation change and conform to what we are speaking over it. Remember, God does not have to *change your situation,* He changes you to be an *agent of change* over your situations!

Impacting My World Confession

I have been blaming others for my actions and felt I had a right to do so. But from now on, I take responsibility for the choices that have me where I am. I confess that I am a leader and am able to make good decisions. I *shall* fulfill my destiny and live better than I ever have before. I call myself blessed and I will be a blessing to my environment. In Jesus' Name, I Declare It! Amen.

What is the Spirit saying to me?

___

He who has an ear, let him hear what the Spirit says...
(Revelation 2:11)

Confession 10

CONSISTENCY

What then shall we say to these things?
(Romans 8:31a)

Daily Word Weapon: II Chronicles 16:9; Psalm 55:17;
II Timothy 2:2, 4:7

God is interested in people who are consistent in their devotion to Him. The life of the believer must conform to the Bible which he claims to believe in. God wants all believers to be dependable, reliable and faithful. He wants us consistent (i.e. "disciplined") so that He can use us to establish His program on earth. The lack of commitment and obedience of many Christians to God makes them undependable. This attracts many setbacks to their lives. Many are so inconsistent in their walk with God that people doubt their conversion and testimony.

Daniel was so consistent in his life and testimony that the leaders of Persia knew he would not change his lifestyle for anything or anyone, even when his life was endangered. Daniel did not get there overnight, but he prayed and gave thanks to God three times each day (Daniel 6:10). The nature of God was greatly imparted through him because of his consistency.

Consistency strengthens the bond of love and fellowship between us and the Father. It guarantees a place in His heart and causes His eyes to be on us all the time. Let God trust you enough to entrust more responsibilities into your hands and boast of you like He boasted about Job (Job 1:6-8). It is often extremely difficult to think or speak spiritually when your flesh or emotions are under attack, if you don't already have it in you.

This is why daily devotion and Bible study are so vital to the believers' survival. You will only say what is in you. You can begin a new consistent walk with the Father today by communing with Him in prayer and immersing yourself daily in His Word. His Word in you will enable you to rise above every life obstacle.

Impacting My World Confession

There is no such thing as I am "too busy", "too tired" or "unable to have personal devotion." The truth of the matter is *I have been too lazy and undisciplined*. I can admit this now, because this is the last day that my old habits keep me from being successful in my future. In Jesus' Name, I Declare It! Amen.

What is the Spirit saying to me?

_____
_____
_____
_____
_____
_____
_____
_____
_____

He who has an ear, let him hear what the Spirit says...
(Revelation 2:11)

Confession 11

MAKING A POSITIVE CONFESSION

*...to **these things**... in **all these things**...*
(Romans 8:31, 37)

Daily Word Weapon: Numbers 14:28;
Deuteronomy 28:13; Hebrews 10:23

We cannot generalize when we are confronting an enemy that is attacking our destiny. Speak *directly* to the thing or things in an authoritative voice! *Don't think it...Whisper...Or ask its permission*! We have got to desire our destiny more than our opposition wants to hinder it! The way we use our mouth will determine if we will overcome the opposition or not, because victory and defeat are in the power of our tongue.

As believers, our confession should be based on the truths of God's Word, instead of just a positive confession. In confessing God's Word, we must not pick out only the scriptures we desire, but also the ones the Lord desires for us. Confessing negative words will create a negative response, but few of us realize that a neutral confession (which is no confession at all), produces the same result as a negative confession. Why? Because the Kingdom of God operates on faith based words! If we want to experience the abundant life that Jesus died to give us, then we have to adopt the method which God has established. God's method of receiving is found in Joshua 1:8, *"Keep this Book of the Law always on your lips; meditate on it day and night, so that you may be careful to do everything written in it. Then you will be prosperous and successful."* This is meditation on God's Word. God has given us the key to receiving what we desire from Him. *Confession brings possession.* We cannot rise above our confession. Our believing is not able to exceed what we are saying out loud. If no words or the wrong words are in our mouth, we are only negating our faith. We need to return to God's way of receiving His blessing. We must begin to speak what God says concerning our life, and allow the creative power behind those words to bring them to reality.

Impacting My World Confession

I confess that God has made me the head and *not* the tail, above only and never beneath. Therefore, I am *never* under the circumstances, under the weather, or feeling a little low. I *am* an overcomer; *over* my past and my fears and *above* average. Supernatural power is at work in my life and the miraculous is my daily bread! In Jesus' Name, I Declare It! Amen.

What is the Spirit saying to me?

_____
_____
_____
_____
_____
_____
_____
_____
_____

He who has an ear, let him hear what the Spirit says...
(Revelation 2:11)

Confession 12

GOD IN YOU

...If God is for us, who can be against us?
(Romans 8:31b)

Daily Word Weapon: Genesis 15:1; Daniel 11:32; Matthew 12:43-45; Ephesians 3:20

We are privileged to come boldly to God's throne to obtain grace for the kingdom responsibility before us. Our uncertainty of where we stand *with* God makes us unable to boldly stand *for* God! The presence of habitual sin, rebellion, deception and other works of darkness, keeps us from having the *blessed assurance* that God will honor our confession. We need to cooperate with God because with Him, all things are possible.

A buildup of sin in a believer's life is always a problem. God has provided a way to clear the accumulation of sin from our lives (I John 1:9), *"If we confess our sins, he is faithful and just and will forgive us our sins and purify us from all unrighteousness."* Unless we confess and forsake our sins, we'll be running on diminished power. This is because the power for living comes from God and not us. When we try to live the christian life in our own strength, we'll feel defeated like windmills robbed of their energy.

God's power can be more easily experienced in our lives when we get rid of sin's buildup every day. If all we do is stop doing what is wrong and just get rid of what is bad, sooner or later, something even worse will fill the void of the old sinfulness. We must replace the bad with God's presence, power and purpose in our lives.

We must pursue Jesus and the character of His kingdom, letting the Holy Spirit fill, empower and make us true instruments of grace in God's hands. God in us is able to do exceedingly, abundantly above what we ask or think, but we must work together with Him in order to perform great exploits for Him.

Impacting My World Confession

I refuse to be plagued by the accusations of my failures. My past, even if it was yesterday...*Today*, it is under the blood! I renounce my secret sins and acts of rebellion that have kept me from being spiritually fulfilled. Today, I embrace a new lease on life. My new beginning starts now! In Jesus' Name, I Declare It! Amen.

What is the Spirit saying to me?

_____
_____
_____
_____
_____
_____
_____
_____
_____
_____

He who has an ear, let him hear what the Spirit says...
(Revelation 2:11)

Confession 13

MY POSITION IN CHRIST

So Jesus answered and said to them, Assuredly, I say to you...
(Matthew 21:21a)

Daily Word Weapon: Psalm 37:1-8; John 16:15;
Ephesians 2:1-10

In walking out our Christian lives, so much of our being able to bridge the gap between what we *see* happen in our lives, and what the Bible *says* is true, comes from what we *believe* and what our *perceptions* of truth are. There is so much power in realizing our position in Christ, because, that is the foundation for us to be able to grow and make progress in our faith. The foundation of our position in Christ is based on what Jesus' shed blood bought for us on the Cross.

Through Jesus' sacrifice, we have been translated into the family of Heaven, where we are able to enter into a personal relationship with Jesus, the Father and the Holy Spirit. *This* relationship is the foundational basis from which our position in Christ springs and it enables the power and blessing of Heaven to flow into our lives. Once we begin to realize our position in Christ, it begins to transform our way of thinking and allows us to walk in a greater level of victory.

Our confidence now resides in our privileged position in Christ. We then have the boldness to proclaim our desires according to God's Word because they will surely come to pass. The confidence to confess a thing is initiated by *Who* it is who has given you the authority!

Jesus Himself makes it personal by using the pronoun *"I"* and makes it specific by directing it to *"You"*! He intends for *you* (me) to receive what He's *giving* as a gift to be used and enjoyed! Fill your mouth with His Word because you have His assurance.

Impacting My World Confession

It is no longer a question of *'can* I confess?' but more of *'will* I confess?' For the power to experience guaranteed results is *in my* mouth to be spoken. Jesus has made available to me *all* that He has and is. I simply have to use *my* mouth to get it. Fear, intimidation and doubt are a thing of the past. *I* have power to produce! In Jesus' Name, I Declare It! Amen.

What is the Spirit saying to me?

_____
_____
_____
_____
_____
_____
_____
_____
_____

He who has an ear, let him hear what the Spirit says...
(Revelation 2:11)

Confession 14

DIVINE CONFIDENCE

...if you have faith and do not doubt...
(Matthew 21:21b)

Daily Word Weapon: Proverbs 3:1-8; Hebrews 4:2;
I John 5:14, 15

It is extremely difficult to operate (confess) in the realm of the unseen (spirit), when the vast majority of us *live* only to gratify the flesh with that which is in the seen (materialistic). *That's* why when things are happening in our natural *sight* world, many cease to function in their faith. Faith must be in God, because He is the only reliable spiritual reality that exists. What is the essence of faith that pleases God? It is trust. Trusting God is what it is all about.

Many will say that they believe *in* God, but not as many will say they *believe* God. God has said many things in His word that are to be taken at face value. *He says* that all humans that do not believe in His Son will face judgment in hell. *He says* that He judged Jesus Christ for the sin of mankind. *He says* that heaven awaits those that simply believe that Jesus' death was for them. Trusting these facts, and throwing ourselves upon Him for salvation, begins a personal relationship with Him.

Our relationship with Him develops as we trust Him more. In the process, our wills become attuned to His, and when we pray, we pray for that which is in accordance with His will. If we determine to trust God in all matters, we must be ready to relinquish the privilege of deciding when, how, and where a circumstance is to be resolved, or a prayer answered. To attain *that* level, we need to soak ourselves in His Presence and His Word. This will make His Word become real to us, and we will have the *divine confidence* to carry out our kingdom responsibilities.

Impacting My World Confession

I no longer move nor am I governed by the events, occurrences, or affairs of everyday life. But I *am* moving by *my* faith on *God's* time toward *my* destiny! With the obstacles I have had to overcome, I *am* where I'm supposed to be…but *not* where I'll remain for long! *My* time for supernatural advance, favor and accomplishments is *now*! In Jesus' Name, I Declare It! Amen.

What is the Spirit saying to me?

_____
_____
_____
_____
_____
_____
_____
_____
_____
_____

He who has an ear, let him hear what the Spirit says…
(Revelation 2:11)

Confession 15

GROWING FAITH

...you will not only do what was done to the fig tree, but also if you say to this mountain...
(Matthew 21:21c)

Daily Word Weapon: Matthew 25:21; Luke 19:11-26; Romans 12:3

When Jesus cursed a fig tree in the presence of His disciples, it did not immediately dry up. At first glance Jesus' action may have seemed without result. However, it provided the opportunity for Him to teach His disciples about the value of faith. They were amazed at the fact that the tree had died simply at His Word. When they asked Him why they were unable to do it, He told them it was because of their unbelief. Many of us would testify that we have believed many times about various things, and our experiences at these times have been less than what is promised here.

Have we really received everything for which we have asked? Because of the occasions when it appears that things fall short of the promises which Jesus makes, we conclude that we do not have enough faith. We worry that even this little amount of faith is beyond us. However, faith is not really a *measurable* commodity. The amount is not really what makes it viable. Faith needs something upon which to stand. Faith is always *in* something.

For instance, when we sit on a chair we are exhibiting faith that the chair will accomplish its purpose. It is not the quantity of faith that causes the action, it is *He* in *Whom* the faith is!

The slightest amount of faith in God will cause Him to act. It is our responsibility to feed our spirit with God's Word and act on it so that our faith can grow. As with anything in life, one is promoted to the next level when he or she has shown that they can handle what's on this current realm. It has *nothing* to do with longevity, age or reward. It is solely based on, *"can you be trusted over a few before you are given charge over much?"*

Impacting My World Confession

I have been angry, jealous and envious of those whom I thought I should have been ahead of. Truthfully, I have been too undisciplined, untrustworthy and inconsistent to have any more than I do. But today, *all of that changes*! I set myself in agreement with God's Word. Excuses and procrastination are not my identity! In Jesus' Name, I Declare It! Amen.

What is the Spirit saying to me?

_____
_____
_____
_____
_____
_____
_____
_____
_____

He who has an ear, let him hear what the Spirit says...
(Revelation 2:11)

Confession 16

USE THE KEYS

Therefore God also has highly exalted Him and given Him the name which is above every name, ¹⁰that at the name of Jesus every knee should bow, of those in heaven, and of those on earth, and of those under the earth.
(Philippians 2:9-10)

Daily Word Weapon: Psalm 103:19-22;
Matthew 16:13-27; John 16:23, 24

If you have been standing around and worrying about what satan is doing, it's time you change your mind. It is time you put satan under your feet! Jesus has already given you all the power and authority you need to do this. He has given you the keys of the kingdom. He has made the promise that whatever you bind on earth shall be bound in heaven. That means you can *speak* the Word and bind evil spirits.

You can speak the Word and release God's angelic forces to work on your behalf. In addition to that, you have been given the power of attorney that enables you to use the mighty Name of Jesus. This is a precious Name that is above every other name in heaven and on earth. Therefore do not waste your time getting upset about the devil. *Take authority over him*, because he has already been defeated.

Bind the wicked spirits that try to destroy you and yours! Set loose the Word of God on earth and enforce it with the precious Name of Jesus. You hold the keys! Learn to use them and before long the devil will be freezing in his tracks, worrying about you. Caution...You have to live a life of holiness for you to effectively use the keys!

The Lord knows those who are His, and, Let everyone who names the name of Christ depart from iniquity (II Timothy 2:19). Thus, it is imperative for you to cleanse yourself from every impurity so that you can be useful for God to establish His kingdom on earth.

Impacting My World Confession

As the Father sent Jesus, so Jesus sends me to go and do everything in His name. I declare that when I use that exalted name of Jesus to pray for the sick, they will be healed. Further, when I use His name against demonic forces, they *will* obey and be subdued by it. In Jesus' Name, I Declare It! Amen.

What is the Spirit saying to me?

_____
_____
_____
_____
_____
_____
_____
_____
_____
_____

He who has an ear, let him hear what the Spirit says...
(Revelation 2:11)

Confession 17

HANG ON

So shall My word be that goes forth from My mouth; it shall not return to Me void, but it shall accomplish what I please, and it shall prosper in the thing for which I sent it.

(Isaiah 55:11)

Daily Word Weapon: I Samuel 3:19; Psalm 19:7-14; II Corinthians 10:3-6

Did you know that the battleground for the problem you are facing right now is in your mind and on your lips? If you will hit satan with the Word and cast the care of the situation over on God, you'll win. Hanging on the Word may not always be easy. Why? Satan knows that if he does not steal it from you, you'll use it to enforce his defeat. Don't be surprised if he sends a wicked spirit to try to exalt itself against God's Word.

If you are sick, he may begin to tell you, "You are not healed. You know that healing's not for today. Even if it were, it would not work for you. It might work for somebody else but not you." *Don't buy it!* Don't start thinking about it. Remember this: *It is the Word that does the work, not the one confessing it.* Our assignment is to confess the Word and believe the Word. *The Word will do the work!*

It will work for any believer who will put it to work. It will work for you just like it worked for Jesus when He walked the earth. Jesus said to the devil, "*It is written!*" No matter what satan tries to tell you, refuse to let go of God's Word. Tell him what is written concerning your situation.

Let the Word fight its own fight. It will whip satan every time.

Impacting My World Confession

My circumstances may not agree with or presently depict what I am believing God for. *I will not give up!*, I will rejoice in the God of my salvation and stand on His promises until I see my desired outcome. In Jesus' Name, I Declare It! Amen.

What is the Spirit saying to me?

_____
_____
_____
_____
_____
_____
_____
_____
_____
_____

He who has an ear, let him hear what the Spirit says...
(Revelation 2:11)

Confession 18

THE FINAL AUTHORITY

God is not a man, that He should lie, nor a son of man, that He should repent. Has He said, and will He not do? Or has He spoken, and will He not make it good?
(Numbers 23:19)

Daily Word Weapon: Psalm 9:1-10; Luke 1:37, 38; II Corinthians 4:7-13

The world is full of uncertainty. Hopeless words of doubt are crying out daily from the radio, television and newspapers. Everything around us appears to be in chaos. If you are a believer, you have the unchanging Word of God to depend on. God has no double standard. He does not say one thing today and something else tomorrow. He is *the same yesterday, today, and forever* (Hebrews 13:8).

If you will make God's Word the final authority in your life, it will give you strength and stability when everything else around you gives way. If you will let what God says resolve the issues of life, you will be confident when others are perplexed and peaceful when others are under pressure.

You will be rising above life's challenges when others are being crushed by it. What does it mean to make the Word of God the final authority? It means *having faith in what He says instead of believing what people say. (Say That Again!)*

It means believing what God says instead of what the devil says. It means having faith in what He says instead of what the circumstances say. Make a decision today to do that.

Resolve in your mind to live by faith, not by sight. Boldly give yourself to the authority of God's Word and there will not be anything in this shaky world that can take your security from you.

Impacting My World Confession

God's Word is a lamp to my feet and a light to my path, therefore I will not give up on everything I am trusting God for. I *will* hold on to the incorruptible Bread of Life. Whatever God says concerning me, He will do it and will not change His mind. In Jesus' Name, I Declare It! Amen.

What is the Spirit saying to me?

_____
_____
_____
_____
_____
_____
_____
_____
_____
_____

He who has an ear, let him hear what the Spirit says...
(Revelation 2:11)

Confession 19

START PLANTING

Having been born again, not of corruptible seed but incorruptible, through the word of God which lives and abides forever.
(I Peter 1:23)

Daily Word Weapon: Psalm 119:9-11; Mark 4:23-32; James 1:2-8

Meditating on God's Word is like planting a seed in the ground. If you will make the effort to plant His Word in your heart, it will grow and bring about a change that will take place *effortlessly*. Just as a seed doesn't release its life until it is planted in the ground, God's Word will not set us free until we get it in our hearts. Having a Bible in our hands or even in our heads is not sufficient. *We need to set aside time for a seed of the Word to germinate in our lives.*

Just because there's nothing visible *above ground* when a seed is planted, does *not* mean the seed is not growing. God's Word works the same way. When we meditate on it for one day, we can't expect to see results the next day. We can't meditate on His Word one day and then live differently the other six days. That's like digging up the seed. No one knows how a seed works, nor does anyone understand how the seed of God's Word planted in our heart works.

The Word is a seed that contains the very life of God. When it is planted in our heart and left there, it will release that life. The only effort on our part is to take the time and make the effort to plant the seed. Then, the godly change effortlessly unfolds as the seed of His Word takes root in our heart.

This is a simple truth that many have not grasped. Many are looking for some spectacular encounter with the Lord that will transform their lives instantly. Don't treat the Word of God like a *book*. It is not! It is a spiritual seed that has the supernatural power to produce the harvest of a lifetime. Start planting today!

Impacting My World Confession

I am planting the seed of God's Word in my life and will hold fast to the confession of it unreservedly. I will plant it in my heart and it will bear good fruit that will make ME an instrument of blessing to my world. In Jesus' Name, I Declare It! Amen.

What is the Spirit saying to me?

_____
_____
_____
_____
_____
_____
_____
_____
_____

He who has an ear, let him hear what the Spirit says...
(Revelation 2:11)

Confession 20

A LITTLE DAILY

…Precept upon precept, precept upon precept, Line upon line, line upon line, Here a little, there a little…

(Isaiah 28:13)

Daily Word Weapon: Luke 13:18-21; I Timothy 4:13-16; II Peter 1:5-11

If we are going to mature in God's kingdom, we are going to do it just like a seed that has been planted in the ground. How does a seed grow? It grows constantly (a little all the time) until it accomplishes what it was created to do. Many of us don't function that way spiritually. We study and pray very hard for a few days and then give up. Then, when some tragedy comes, we make a rush attempt to pray and stand on the Word! Then when we do obtain the desired results, or we are not as strong as we ought to be, we are "quick" to give up on God and go back to carnal rationale.

There is no such thing as an instant success in the kingdom of God! Genuine strength and growth comes as you consistently and constantly keep the Word before your eyes, in your ears, and in your heart. Not just when you want to or when you feel like it, but constantly, like the seed, a little all the time. God has a glorious destiny planned for us, but *the daily responsibility to make it a reality is in our hands.*

Therefore, make up your mind to begin that daily process of constant growth today.

Determine to start putting the Word in your heart consistently. Begin to act as though that Word is true every hour of the day, regardless of what comes or how you feel. Keep adding to your faith, meditating on it, confessing it, every day of the week. In the long run, your faith will be bigger than you ever comprehended, and you will be a force to be reckoned with in the kingdom of God.

Impacting My World Confession

Daily will I *wholly* present myself to God to pray and meditate on His Word. In so doing, I will be transformed to know God's will for my life and my progress will be evident to all. In Jesus' Name, I Declare It! Amen.

What is the Spirit saying to me?

___

___

___

___

___

___

___

___

___

___

He who has an ear, let him hear what the Spirit says...
(Revelation 2:11)

Confession 21

INSIDE OUT

But we all, with unveiled face, beholding as in a mirror the glory of the Lord, are being transformed into the same image from glory to glory, just as by the Spirit of the Lord.

(II Corinthians 3:18)

Daily Word Weapon: Genesis 2:21-25; Psalm 8; Isaiah 60:1-6

Have you ever thought about the fact that man is the only creature God created who has to cover himself with clothing? All the other creatures grow their own coverings. Some grow fur, some feathers, and others scales, but all are clothed from the inside out! Most people don't realize it, but in the beginning, man was clothed that way too. He was made in the image of God. If you look in Ezekiel 8:2 (NIV), you'll find that God is clothed in *fire* from the loins up and from the loins down.

I looked, and I saw a figure like that of a man. From what appeared to be his waist down he was like fire, and from there up his appearance was as bright as glowing metal.

That *fire* is His glory emanating outward from His innermost being. When man was first created, he was like that too. He was covered with the very glory of God. It radiated from his inner being outwardly. That's why he had no sense of nakedness until after he sinned and the glory departed from him. As you gaze into the Lord's face by studying the Word and fellowshipping with Him; as you renew your mind to understand who you are in Christ, you will be changed into His image on the outside as well.

As you learn to hear His voice and obey it, you will start giving an outward expression of the glory within you. Gradually, you'll be turned inside out! Instead of simply staring into your closet every morning, spend some time gazing at Jesus and beholding His Word. Let Him clothe you in His radiant presence. Once His glory starts shining through, anything you wear will look beautiful on you.

Impacting My World Confession

I present myself to You and will always abide in Your Word. I declare that my life is transformed and conformed into the image of my Lord Jesus Christ as I immerse myself in His Word. In Jesus' Name, I Declare It! Amen.

What is the Spirit saying to me?

___

He who has an ear, let him hear what the Spirit says...
(Revelation 2:11)

Confession 22

WALK IN THE LIGHT

But you must continue in the things which you have learned and been assured of, knowing from whom you have learned them.
(II Timothy 3:14)

Daily Word Weapon: James 1:22; I Peter 4:10, 11;
II Peter 1:2-11

If you are born again and have God's Word in your heart, you can live in victory. You may not have all the answers, and there may be many spiritual things that you still don't understand. However, it is not those things that are most likely to destroy you. What destroys are the things that you *know* to do, but *don't* carry out. These are the things that usually make you fall. Just think about walking down a dark, unfamiliar path in the middle of a jungle. Your guide up ahead has a flashlight to keep you on the right path.

That's exactly the same thing that can happen in your walk with God. He knows what's ahead and He shines just enough light for you to take one step at a time. You have to continue walking in *that* light in order to arrive at where you are going. You may not know why He is leading you in a certain way, but you must learn to *trust His heart* even when you can't *trace His hand*!

You may not understand all the things involved, but God will make up for your ignorance through the guidance of the Holy Spirit. He'll see to it that you have victory if you continue in what you know. It's good to keep studying. It's good to keep learning. Remember, it is not the great revelation you haven't yet grasped that will cause you the most trouble. It's failing to walk in the ones God has already revealed to you. So be faithful in those things. Continue in them day after day after day. You'll make it through just fine!

Impacting My World Confession

Father! I will walk in the light you have revealed to me because, therein lies my profiting and fruitfulness. I *will be* a good steward of Your revelation in my care and will continue in Your Word so that I can bear much fruit. In Jesus' Name, I Declare It! Amen.

What is the Spirit saying to me?

_____
_____
_____
_____
_____
_____
_____
_____
_____
_____

He who has an ear, let him hear what the Spirit says...
(Revelation 2:11)

Confession 23

HOLINESS IS A LIFESTYLE

He who has My commandments and keeps them, it is he who loves Me. And he who loves Me will be loved by My Father, and I will love him and manifest Myself to him.

(John 14:21)

Daily Word Weapon: Ephesians 1:1-6;
I Thessalonians 4:1-8; I Peter 1:13-21

There is a dimension of living you can only experience when you make a decision to please the Father in everything. In *that* dimension, Jesus becomes real to you and manifests Himself to you. Just after the turn of the century, God poured out His Spirit on a group of people and started a revival on Azusa Street. It was an awesome time, a time when people's lives were radically changed by the power of the Holy Ghost.

Everything else in their world seemed to lose importance, because God was manifesting Himself greatly in their presence. The people involved in that revival began to be known to the world as *holiness people*. They got that title because they were so *obviously different* from everyone else. Few Christians today know what holiness means, and very few understand the outpouring of God that comes to those who *dare* to step into it.

This lifestyle is only possible when we "put on" His nature of holiness. We can only do this by *feeding* on the Word of God to develop this grace. What is holiness? It simply means being *separated to God*. It is what you do with your life day by day. It is when you conduct yourself according to God's Word and the promptings of His Spirit. Holiness is a lifestyle of being one mind with God; of turning away from the ways of the world and living instead in agreement with Him. Living a life of holiness does *not* happen by accident. It requires a *decision of the will*. Make that decision today. Love God with all your heart by keeping His commandments. He will show you His love by making Himself known to you in unimaginable new ways. He will *pour* Himself out on you just like He did on those believers at Azusa Street, and revival will truly begin in you.

Impacting My World Confession

Today, I purge myself from any impurities that try to prevent my communion with my Heavenly Father. From now on, I declare that I will experience the times of refreshing that only come from spending time in His presence. As I do this, I continually receive His divine power, so that I can be a partaker of His divine nature. By so doing, I live a life of purity *without struggle*. In Jesus' Name I Declare It! Amen.

What is the Spirit saying to me?

___

He who has an ear, let him hear what the Spirit says...
(Revelation 2:11)

Confession 24

LIVING A LIFE OF LOVE

But whoever keeps His word, truly the love of God is perfected in him. By this we know that we are in Him. ⁶He who says he abides in Him ought himself also to walk just as He walked.

(I John 2:5, 6)

Daily Word Weapon: I Corinthians 13:1-3;
I Peter 4:7, 8; I John 4:7-21

There is absolutely nothing that is more important than learning to walk in love. Indeed, how accurately we perfect our *love walk* will determine how much of God's "perfect will" we will get done. That's because, every other spiritual force derives its action from love. For instance, the Bible teaches us that faith works by love (I Corinthians 13:2). Answered prayer is impossible when a believer steps outside of love and refuses to forgive or is in strife with his brother or sister (Psalm 66:17,18).

Without love, our giving will not bring forth the right harvest. In the absence of love, tongues and prophecy will amount to nothing, faith fails and knowledge is unfruitful. All the truths that we have learned from God's Word work by love. They will profit us nothing unless we walk in love. I Corinthians 13:4-8 paints a perfect picture of how *love* behaves. It is patient and kind. It is not jealous or proud. It does not behave rudely or selfishly and it is not easily offended. Love "bears all things, believes all things, hopes all things, and endures all things."

Sounds like a tall order, doesn't it? Don't despair. You are a *love creation*. God has recreated your spirit in the image of love. He has sent His Spirit of love to live inside of you and teach you how to love as He loves. *You can live the love life.* Why not ask Him to help you to begin today?

Impacting My World Confession

Because God *is* love, and I am created in the image of God, I walk in love at all times! Jesus gave His life for me, and by the grace and the Spirit of God in me, I love my fellow brothers and sisters unconditionally. I am a disciple of Jesus Christ. The world will know my relationship with *Him* by the love I demonstrate towards *them*. In Jesus' Name I Declare It! Amen!

What is the Spirit saying to me?

_____
_____
_____
_____
_____
_____
_____
_____
_____

He who has an ear, let him hear what the Spirit says...
(Revelation 2:11)

Confession 25

THE ROCK OF OUR SALVATION

The LORD is my rock and my fortress and my deliverer; my God, my strength, in whom I will trust; my shield and the horn of my salvation, my stronghold.

(Psalm 18:2)

Daily Word Weapon: I Samuel 30:6; Psalm 27; 42:1-5

The greatness of a person lies in his ability to find something or someone else stronger than him to lean on. God, "the Rock of our Salvation," understands and knows our need for receiving encouragement. Many times, insurmountable circumstances may try to *discourage* our souls. At other times, the negative words of those we love or those we look up to, may discourage us. Sometimes the *journey* to reach a goal is so long – almost like climbing Mount Everest or trekking to the South or North Pole all by yourself - it can cause one to become discouraged.

If something were easy or convenient to do, every Tom, Dick and Harry would be doing it. Those who succeed find something stronger than themselves to lean on or to draw their strength from. The Word of God is to be our source of daily life and strength. Joshua, while being told to be strong and of good courage, was also told to meditate on the Word of God daily (Joshua 1:5-9). It is alright to feel the emotion of discouragement but you must never let these emotions *rule* you. Feel the feeling, but go on any how! You must *tap* into your spirit man where God, through His spirit, has poured love, joy, peace, longsuffering, gentleness, goodness, faithfulness, meekness and temperance (Galatians 5:22-23). Treat discouragement as the soul's *hunger pangs* for God's Word. If you have not eaten for some time, your stomach growls and makes noises. In like manner, if you have not drawn from the strength of your inner man and spirit, your *soul man* makes negative *emotional* noises. Spend time with the Lord and in His Word, then your soul will be living in encouragement, love, rest and contentment in God.

Impacting My World Confession

I surrender to You O Lord! I make a firm decision to stop toiling and I release my will to *Your* leading. I thirst for You O God and make a decision to go all the way with You. Satisfy my longing soul and take me deeper in You. Take me to the depths of love that I have not known and the heights of joy that I long to reach. In Jesus' Name I Declare It! Amen!

What is the Spirit saying to me?

___

He who has an ear, let him hear what the Spirit says...
(Revelation 2:11)

Confession 26

WAITING ON THE LORD

But those who wait on the LORD shall renew their strength; they shall mount up with wings like eagles, they shall run and not be weary, they shall walk and not faint.

(Isaiah 40:31)

Daily Word Weapon: Psalm 27:13, 14; 92; 103:1-5

Did you know that the *force of faith* has the power to invigorate your physical body? It is true. You can see this in the life of Abraham's wife, Sarah. Most people don't understand the full extent of what God did in her life. All they know is that He enabled her to have a child in her old age. If you look closer, you will see that there was more to it than that. When Sarah believed the promise of God, it began to restore her physically, making her younger. So much so that, when King Abimelech saw her, he wanted her for his wife!

Think about that! At 90 years old, she was so beautiful that a king wanted her in his harem (Genesis 20-21). What's more, after she gave birth to Isaac, she nursed him till he was weaned. Then she kept right on living until that boy was raised! Now, I am not saying that you can have a baby at 90 like Sarah did. She had a specific promise from God about that. But what I *am* telling you is, that, if you'll believe God for renewed strength and health in any stage of your life, He'll provide it for you.

God's desire for you in your old age is that you are powerful, an experienced champion of His Word with your strength renewed by faith. Wait on Him. Start to confess that today. Fill your mouth with His promises and declare them until you see your desired manifestation. You will still go to heaven when your work on earth is through, but you don't have to just *fade away*. You will fly out of here in a blaze of glory like the conqueror God created you to be. Therefore, wait on Him always!

Impacting My World Confession

Father! You are my hope and my salvation. I don't have any other alternative, hence, I will wait on You. My strength will be renewed and my mouth will be satisfied with Your goodness all the days of my life. In Jesus' Name I Declare It! Amen!

What is the Spirit saying to me?

___

___

___

___

___

___

___

___

___

He who has an ear, let him hear what the Spirit says...
(Revelation 2:11)

Confession 27

PURITY OF HEART

Blessed are the pure in heart, for they shall see God.

(Matthew 5:8)

Daily Word Weapon: Psalm 15; Philippians 3:7-11; I John 2:3-11

Christianity is not just a set of rules, creeds and theology. It does include all these things. However, the most marvelous revelation is that, it is a *direct relationship* with God our Father and the Lord Jesus Christ *through* the Holy Spirit. The whole concept of eternal life is the privilege of knowing God. Whatever our Christian life on earth, whatever our ministry life on earth and whatever our earthly positions or status, the greatest achievement we could aspire to while on earth is to *know* God.

This is the purpose for which we were born and the very essence of our creation and existence. This short life on earth was designed that through all of the circumstances and experiences that we have in our lives, that we might come to know God and love God. By so doing, we will then be able to love our neighbor as ourselves. We can know about everything on earth but if we miss learning to know God, we have missed everything. Knowing God involves opening all of our being to Him, and the first place to start is always in our hearts. God is Spirit and only through our spirit can we know God.

God *is* light and only when we are *in* the light can we see Him. It is impossible to deceive God because darkness fades in the light of God's righteousness. It is possible for us to experience and see more through the eyes of our heart when we bring ourselves in alignment with love towards God and towards others. This can be done by daily presenting ourselves as a living sacrifice to God through meditation on His Word. By so doing, our spiritual eyes are opened and we are transformed to know God progressively.

Impacting My World Confession

Father! I surrender myself to You. Purify me from sin with hyssop, and I will be clean. Wash me, and I will be whiter than snow. I am willing to receive, and to keep my spiritual eyes opened, so that I can perceive and receive all that You have for me. In Jesus' Name I Declare It! Amen!

What is the Spirit saying to me?

_____
_____
_____
_____
_____
_____
_____
_____
_____
_____

He who has an ear, let him hear what the Spirit says...
(Revelation 2:11)

Confession 28

FAITH AND HOLINESS

But without faith it is impossible to please Him, for he who comes to God must believe that He is, and that He is a rewarder of those who diligently seek Him.

(Hebrews 11:6)

Daily Word Weapon: I Corinthians 9:24-27; Hebrews 12:14; I Peter 1:13-16

We can only live a successful life of holiness when it grows from an inner belief to an *outer lifestyle*. *This* is the part where faith comes into play. Since holiness is a gift, then it is also dependent on our faith level to appropriate it. As always, faith to appropriate holiness is different from faith to appropriate other areas of spiritual and natural life. We need to understand *how* to exercise faith for holiness as much as in all other areas of life.

Faith *draws from* the spirit continually and allows it to *flow through* the soul, to be manifested in the body. The mind must remain conscious of the union of our spirit to the Spirit of Christ within us, while the body needs to be *pummeled* to be led by the Spirit in holiness. Faith holds on to the perception of the transformed mind. It takes faith to see that sin is ugly. It takes faith to see that holiness is beautiful.

The Holy Spirit renews our mind to see beauty in holiness and find true spiritual beauty. *Faith eyes* see the possibility of the right kind of beauty in everything. By faith we must learn to put on the new man which is created in righteousness and holiness. *This* new man is that which was created when Christ came into our hearts.

By faith we learn to put off the old man and put on the new man. The journey to a consistent life of holiness starts when we *regularly* purge ourselves from the impurities that slow us down and focus on Christ (The Word). Then our faith for holiness increases, and thus, holiness becomes our normal way of life.

Impacting My World Confession

By the power of the Holy Spirit, I purpose to purge myself of every sin and iniquity that slows me down in my *journey* of purpose. By faith, I put on the new man which is created in righteousness and continually live a holy life. I am enabled to do this by Christ who lives inside of me. In Jesus' Name I Declare It! Amen!

What is the Spirit saying to me?

_____
_____
_____
_____
_____
_____
_____
_____
_____

He who has an ear, let him hear what the Spirit says...
(Revelation 2:11)

Confession 29

THE CLOTHING OF POWER

Behold, I send the Promise of My Father upon you; but tarry in the city of Jerusalem until you are endued with power from on high.

(Luke 24:49)

Daily Word Weapon: Psalm 84:7; John 15:1-5; Acts 1:4-8

It is imperative that we do what is necessary in our walk with God to ensure that we are flowing with maximum power in our lives. Although the Almighty God has placed in each of us our divine destinies, within each call, there can be variations of the Holy Ghost's power. A lack of understanding in how to flow with this power or pure laziness in walking in the laws of the spirit, can determine the magnitude to which the spirit releases this power. There are keys which must be included in a Christian life to ensure that this power is maintained or increased.

First, *a life of prayer and fasting is necessary.* Our Lord Jesus was accustomed to spending much time in prayer. His disciples must have been greatly impressed with His prayer life, in so much as they asked Him to teach them to pray (Luke 11:1). Secondly, *learning to walk with the Holy Spirit* will also help a great deal. Walking closely with the Holy Spirit means walking in the love of God. Our hearts will be full of God's love and our mouths filled with His praises when we are filled with the Holy Spirit.

It takes meditation on God's Word and worship to bring the presence of the Holy Spirit from our closet into our daily lives and routine. Thirdly, *being filled with God's Word* will also help maintain a life of power. Obviously, for a person to be filled with faith, that person would have to be full of the Word of God. We can never evangelize the world by our own strength or organizational ability. Like the call of Jesus to His disciples, the call of the Spirit is that we do not leave our prayer closets until we have been endued with power from on high.

Impacting My World Confession

Father! I come boldly to Your Throne to receive the daily impartation of grace for the task before me. Without You I can do nothing, therefore I will wait on You to receive *Your* power so that I can impact *my* generation for You. In Jesus' Name I Declare It! Amen!

What is the Spirit saying to me?

___

___

___

___

___

___

___

___

___

___

He who has an ear, let him hear what the Spirit says...
(Revelation 2:11)

Confession 30

PRESS IN!

Let the word of Christ dwell in you richly in all wisdom, teaching and admonishing one another in psalms and hymns and spiritual songs, singing with grace in your hearts to the Lord.

(Colossians 3:16)

Daily Word Weapon: Psalm 119:9-16; John 1:1-14; Philippians 3:12-16

Things in this world are not getting better, and in recent times, the Holy Spirit has been speaking urgently to many believers. He has been saying, "Press in. Draw into a more intimate relationship with your Heavenly Father. If you don't, you will not make it. If you do, you will see more glorious outpourings of Me than you can imagine." The message is for every believer on earth today. We are in the last of the last days of this age.

Jesus is coming soon. It is an exciting time, but it is also a dangerous time. Those who don't yield to the Spirit and who don't press into God, are going to go from tragedy to tragedy. Those who do will defeat the tragedies and finish gloriously. Your first step in drawing closer to God is to realize that you know Him in His Word.

Time spent meditating in the New Testament is time spent with Jesus. Most people don't realize that. So, instead of getting to know the Lord through His Word, they try to know Him through their feelings ... *that just won't work.*

Letting the Word dominate your thinking is to *allow the Holy Spirit to have control over your mind.* As you do that, your feelings will eventually fall in line with His Word.

Remember this, John 1:1-14, says that Jesus is the Word. That means, when you spend time *in* it, you are spending time in Him! When His Word is dwelling in you richly, then Jesus is dwelling in you richly too! Don't go from tragedy to tragedy. Use those adversities to your advantage. Press into Jesus. Press into His Word and you'll make it through these dangerous days just fine!

Impacting My World Confession

Today, I purpose to forget all my past experiences. I desperately seek after God, reaching forward to those things which are ahead. I will no longer settle for the beggarly "crumbs" of life's existence. Abundance is my portion. I *will* have all that has been promised for me through the death of my Lord. In Jesus' Name I Declare It! Amen!

What is the Spirit saying to me?

___

He who has an ear, let him hear what the Spirit says...
(Revelation 2:11)

Confession 31

DAILY DEPENDENCE ON GOD

One thing I have desired of the LORD, That will I seek: That I may dwell in the house of the LORD all the days of my life, to behold the beauty of the LORD, and to inquire in His temple. ⁵For in the time of trouble He shall hide me in His pavilion; In the secret place of His tabernacle He shall hide me; He shall set me high upon a rock.
(Psalm 27:4-5)

Daily Word Weapon: Psalm 91; John 15:1-8; Philippians 2:12-16

When you rise in the morning, do you feel helpless, and in need of strength from God? Do you humbly and heartily make known your wants to your Heavenly Father? Paul the Apostle both learned and mastered this key to the secret of daily dependence on God's unlimited supply of strength. Once he had done this, he could declare that he now took pleasure in all the various circumstances (infirmities) that normally defeat mankind (II Corinthians 12:10).

By examining the *fall from grace* of the Galatians, it is noted that they were no longer walking in faith and love, but in the works of the law. Therein lies the secret to tapping into the daily unlimited supply of God's strength. First and foremost, one must have the motivation of *unconditional love* towards God and others. When love is the only reason and motivation for doing what we do, there is no end to the supply of God's strength to accomplish anything, for we will be in complete synergy with God, who is love.

Each day as you go about your business, acknowledge that you can't do it in your own strength, but God can. Depend completely on God for *His* strength - not your own. Throw yourself into the arms of Jesus and ask Him to carry you as you do the work that He has called you to do. As you begin to see success, don't forget that it is God who strengthens you and provides the ability for you to do the work. He is the One who must be acknowledged in the midst of your success.

Impacting My World Confession

Father! I let go of my self-sufficiency and come to a place of Your rest. *You* are my sufficiency. Wrap me in your arms and take me to Your secret place where I can be with you. Here is where I can find strength for the day and the journey before me. In Jesus' Name I Declare It! Amen!

What is the Spirit saying to me?

_____
_____
_____
_____
_____
_____
_____
_____
_____
_____

He who has an ear, let him hear what the Spirit says...
(Revelation 2:11)

Confession 32

THE SANCTIFIED LIFE

Now may the God of peace Himself sanctify you completely; and may your whole spirit, soul, and body be preserved blameless at the coming of our Lord Jesus Christ.
(I Thessalonians 5:23)

Daily Word Weapon: John 17:17; Romans 12:1, 2;
I Thessalonians 4:3-5

Living a daily sanctified life implies a *letting go* of worldly motivations in our lives. The goal of sanctification is one of beauty. Hence, once we are sanctified in our heart, mind and body, we become beautiful in our spirit, soul and outer life. Moral uprightness without mental and heart purity is not true sanctification. On the other hand, mental and heart sanctification will always produce moral uprightness. All sin springs from our heart and in our mind before it is acted out. We cannot overcome sin by willpower, we can only overcome it by God's power.

By allowing the grace of God's pure love to energize and motivate us in our day to day affairs, we live a sanctified life that pleases God. Strive to do everything out of love for God and sin will be banished out of your life. This can be achieved by *practicing the presence of God*. Through this, we live a life of holiness (without struggle) because we are filled with His fullness.

Knowing that we are *in* the world but not *of* the world, Jesus prayed that we might be sanctified by the truth of His Word. Jesus sanctified Himself that we might be sanctified by the truth. Jesus had the pure motive of love flowing through Him twenty-four hours a day when He was on the earth and sought nothing of this temporal world. We are His disciples and He now lives within us. As such, we should allow the same purity of love to direct every detail of our lives. We are sanctified in Him.

Impacting My World Confession

Father! I confess my sins and forsake my sinful habit. I will daily present myself as a living sacrifice, holy and acceptable to You. As I do, I declare that I am washed clean by Your Word. In Jesus' Name I Declare It! Amen!

What is the Spirit saying to me?

_____
_____
_____
_____
_____
_____
_____
_____
_____
_____

He who has an ear, let him hear what the Spirit says...
(Revelation 2:11)

Confession 33

CHRIST: THE WAY OF LIFE

But of Him you are in Christ Jesus, who became for us wisdom from God - and righteousness and sanctification and redemption.
(I Corinthians 1:30)

Daily Word Weapon: John 14:6; I Corinthians 3:11; I Peter 3:15

There is a vast difference between knowledge and wisdom. It is possible to have knowledge yet lack wisdom. Every time we hear a sermon or read a good book, we immediately receive knowledge but not necessarily wisdom. If the sermon or book contains wisdom and truth, then by meditating upon and applying what is newly acquired, it will, through time, become our conviction and lifestyle.

Christianity is not about *what we know*, it is about *who we are*. If all Christians were to put to practice what they already know in Christ, this world would be different. Whenever we find some knowledge and truth that resonates within our spirit, it is beneficial that we go over it from time to time until our spirit absorbs its truth. *This* is the essence of meditation. Through this, it becomes part of our heart and not just our head.

Meditating on the truths of God once in a while may not be sufficient. Those truths that resonate within our spirit need to be repeatedly read and meditated upon until they become a part of our subconscious, and then a part of our lives. God's Word is not merely meant for the impartation of truth and knowledge, but also for the very transformation of our lives into the full glory of Christ. The wise man builds on the right foundation – which is the foundation of Christ. This means that he also depends on the strength of Christ to be a doer and not just his own strength.

Impacting My World Confession

Jesus, because You live in me, I declare that I will grow stronger in Your strength in me day by day as I commune with You. Today, I purpose for my relationship with You to grow deeper through the revelation of Your abounding love. In Jesus' Name I Declare It! Amen!

What is the Spirit saying to me?

___

He who has an ear, let him hear what the Spirit says...
(Revelation 2:11)

Confession 34

A VESSEL UNTO HONOR

But in a great house there are not only vessels of gold and silver, but also of wood and clay, some for honor and some for dishonor.
(II Timothy 2:20)

Daily Word Weapon: Isaiah 60:1; II Corinthians 6:11-18; II Timothy 2:15-26

Are you destined for greatness in the kingdom of God? Quite a few believers will respond that they are not. They would say, "we can't all be precious vessels." Certainly there are going to be some golden vessels in the kingdom and there are going to be some clay pots. However, *we* are the ones, *not God*, who determine which we will be. Becoming a precious vessel in God's hands requires that we separate ourselves from contaminating and corrupting influences.

This is imperative so that we can be useful for honorable and noble purposes, consecrated and profitable to the Master. The choice is ours whether to be a vessel unto honor or dishonor. Why then do so many believers choose to do basic work in the kingdom of God? Why are they content to remain *clay pots*? This is because they lack one thing every precious vessel must have... *dedication*. They have not made a quality decision to separate themselves from contaminating influences. They have not been willing to *turn away from* the ways of the world and *go on with* God past the point of no return.

God is doing some exciting things in the earth realm right now. He is working signs and wonders, paving the way for Jesus' return.

This *is* a thrilling time, but it's definitely no time for clay pots! So if you have not yet made the kind of commitment that will turn you into a golden vessel, admit it. Then take the time to get before God and study His Word and align your will with His. Make a decision now because the night is far spent and the day is at hand. Tomorrow may be too late!

Impacting My World Confession

Today, I cast off every work of darkness in my life and put on the armor of light. I confess that I *am* a vessel of honor through which God's gifts and fruit can operate. I refuse to be a normal Christian, living an average life and receiving the "leftovers" of what has been promised to me. In Jesus' Name I Declare It! Amen!

What is the Spirit saying to me?

_____
_____
_____
_____
_____
_____
_____
_____
_____

He who has an ear, let him hear what the Spirit says...
(Revelation 2:11)

Confession 35

EQUIPPED TO WIN

I have written to you, fathers, because you have known Him who is from the beginning. I have written to you, young men, because you are strong, and the word of God abides in you, and you have overcome the wicked one.
(I John 2:14)

Daily Word Weapon: Joshua 1:1-9; Romans 8:31-39; I John 5:1-5

God created man to be a winner. We read in Genesis, for example, that man was originally put on this earth to have dominion over all other creatures. God gave him authority over the earth and everything that crept, flew, crawled, and breathed there. Man did not know what defeat was until he separated himself from his Source through disobedience in the Garden of Eden. When that happened, he ran headlong into defeat.

He was forced to accept failure as his lot in life, lowering himself to a subordinate position. This is a sad story. Nevertheless, if you are a born again child of God, your story has a happy ending. Through faith in Christ Jesus, we have been made a winner once again! In fact, God has *guaranteed* your success. Let me show you what I mean. Imagine you are about to embark on a venture, and before you get started, God speaks to you out loud and says, "I just want you to know, I am going to personally see to it that this project you are working on succeeds."

Does that mean you won't have any more trouble in the process? No. It simply means you can go through that trouble and emerge triumphant. If you have been feeling like a failure lately, renew your mind by the Word of God that says you are a success. Every time a challenge comes up, respond by saying, "Well, praise God, I can overcome this obstacle because I am an overcomer in Jesus!" Let that Word from God abide in your heart. It *will* make a winner out of you.

Impacting My World Confession

Jesus, You are the High Priest over my confession and You watch over Your Word to perform it. Therefore I declare that I am fearfully and wonderfully made by You! I am made to be victorious. I strip away every unnecessary weight and every sin from my life. I run this race with patience and I run this race to win. I rule and reign in this life through Christ Jesus. In Jesus' Name I Declare It! Amen!

What is the Spirit saying to me?

___

He who has an ear, let him hear what the Spirit says...
(Revelation 2:11)

Confession 36

MINISTERING FROM THE OVERFLOW

If you abide in Me, and My words abide in you, you will ask what you desire, and it shall be done for you. [8]By this My Father is glorified, that you bear much fruit; so you will be My disciples.
(John 15:7-8)

Daily Word Weapon: Psalm 23; Mark 5:18-20; I John 4:7-16

The vessels of God can be categorized into three groups; those who are *not yet* filled, those who *are* filled and, those who *continually receive the inflow* while they are filled. This allows them to overflow, making deposits into the lives of others. Imagine a cup that is in the process of being filled; it can be completely filled to the brim or it can be overflowing. A cup can contain some water, or it can be filled with water, or it can be completely immersed in water.

It is the third position to be overflowing or totally immersed in the Spirit of God that we should be in before we minister. We not only must receive the Spirit within us, we must be completely covered and immersed in the Spirit. When the Spirit fills us until we overflow, we are enabled to minister in the name of our Lord. How easy would it be to minister from the overflow? Extremely easy because there would be no effort on our part.

It would be all Him (Jesus) flowing (moving) through our yielded lives. This overflow needs to be maintained daily by spending quality time with God, meditation on His Word, coupled with prayer and worship.

Basically, it simply means staying connected with God by way of your spirit man, even while you are going about your life's work. Through this spiritual connection and union with God, you can discern between when you are filled from when you need to be filled and when you are overflowing with His Spirit and His Word. Every time you sense that you are not filled, you should draw nigh to Him and draw from Him as your source, until your rivers and fountains are flowing again.

Impacting My World Confession

Jesus, I abide in You, and Your Word abides in me. I am filled with the Holy Spirit and I move in a fresh anointing to be a witness for You and share my testimony. I am anointed to be an ambassador of Christ, representing Him in the earth and helping others to be reconciled to God. In Jesus' Name I Declare It! Amen!

What is the Spirit saying to me?

_____
_____
_____
_____
_____
_____
_____
_____
_____

He who has an ear, let him hear what the Spirit says...
(Revelation 2:11)

Confession 37

SPEAK LIKE GOD

For assuredly, I say to you, whoever says to this mountain, 'Be removed and be cast into the sea,' and does not doubt in his heart, but believes that those things he says will be done, he will have whatever he says.

(Mark 11:23)

Daily Word Weapon: Genesis 2:19, 20; Mark 11:12-23; Romans 4:13-25

Jesus did not say, "Whosoever shall speak to God about this mountain." He said *we should speak what we desire directly to the mountain*. From a worldly point of view, that sounds foolish. However, I Corinthians 1:27 makes it clear that God has chosen the foolish things of the world to confound the wise. It is always going to sound foolish to the world when a Christian talks as if what God has promised is a reality, especially when those promises seem to contradict the natural evidence around us.

If you want to *keep* the devil defeated, that is the kind of talking we must be engaged in. The Bible says that God Himself talks that way! Romans 4:17(KJV) states that, *"God calleth those things which be not as though they were."* God does not wait for circumstances to line up before He speaks. He *causes* them to line up *because* He speaks. You can do the same thing if you will make your words agree with His and speak them out of *your* mouth by faith.

You may ask, "What if nothing happens right away?" or "What if the circumstances don't immediately change?" When Jesus spoke to that fig tree in Mark 11:14, He did not go back and check to see if anything had happened to it. No, once He had spoken it, He considered it done. Then, a day later, He and His disciples *saw* the impact of His *words*. Follow His example. Let your faith speak. Agree with God's Word!

Impacting My World Confession

I am created in the image of God and have His nature. As a result of this, whatever I say with my mouth will come to pass. Therefore, I proclaim that I fly above every mountain of poverty, failure, barrenness, fruitless efforts, and sorrow. I declare that I am moving from victory to victory, power to power, success to success and glory to glory. In Jesus' Name I Declare It! Amen!

What is the Spirit saying to me?

___

___

___

___

___

___

___

___

He who has an ear, let him hear what the Spirit says...
(Revelation 2:11)

Confession 38

DOING THE WORKS OF JESUS

Most assuredly, I say to you, he who believes in Me, the works that I do he will do also; and greater works than these he will do, because I go to My Father.

(John 14:12)

Daily Word Weapon: John 14:7-24; 15:5; II Timothy 2:20-22

It is the desire of our Lord Jesus that we bear much fruit for Him. This is done not through our own strength, for in ourselves we can do nothing. However, *through* Christ *in* us we can do all things. We were especially ordained and chosen to be productive in all things assigned to us by God. Jesus revealed that the secret to His success in all of His works on earth, was through the indwelling of the Father in Him. Our ability to do His works and greater works is based on Him going to His Father. The phrase 'going to the Father' was completed in the revelation that when He had gone to the Father, He would send the Holy Spirit who is *with* us and *in* us.

Through the Holy Spirit, we fully understand the power of the union that we have in Christ. The success seen in the works of Jesus and the greater works He declared concerning us, is in the power of He being in the Father and the Father in Him and then of His Spirit dwelling in us. We should therefore take time everyday to meditate on the indwelling of Christ and God within us. This is the same power within us that Paul speaks about by which God can work mightily *above what we think or ask*.

All the works that God would have us do on earth have already been foreordained and pre-planned by God. We need to be in union with Christ for these works to flow through us. We can do this by embracing His Word and allowing Him to dwell in us through His Word. Do not struggle to do the greater works of God but rather, let the greater works of God flow through you.

Impacting My World Confession

I have been crucified with Christ. Jesus lives in me and works through me because I am a branch in the vine (Him). Therefore, I receive His life and strength, and become His workmanship *created* for good works. In Jesus' Name I Declare It! Amen!

What is the Spirit saying to me?

_____
_____
_____
_____
_____
_____
_____
_____
_____

He who has an ear, let him hear what the Spirit says...
(Revelation 2:11)

Confession 39

OCCUPY UNTIL JESUS COMES

Therefore take up the whole armor of God, that you may be able to withstand in the evil day, and having done all, to stand. [14] Stand therefore, having girded your waist with truth, having put on the breastplate of righteousness, [15] and having shod your feet with the preparation of the gospel of peace; [16] above all, taking the shield of faith with which you will be able to quench all the fiery darts of the wicked one. [17] And take the helmet of salvation, and the sword of the Spirit, which is the word of God.

(Ephesians 6:13-17)

Daily Word Weapon: Luke 11:14-23; 12:35-44; II Timothy 2:1-5

The Bible teaches that as believers, we should *occupy* until Jesus comes. Occupy is a military term meaning to "hold possession of, or control conquered troops and territory." However, if we are to do that effectively, most of us are going to have to change our attitudes. We are going to have to recognize that Jesus has already won the victory. *That's right. Satan is already defeated!* He was defeated on the cross of Calvary.

We are not on the defensive, *he* is! What is more, Jesus has given us His very own armor and sword to use, to keep our defeated foe in line. You may be a ninety pound weakling on your own, but if you will put on the armor of God, the devil will never know it. He will run from you as if you were Jesus. Think about it, He is terrified of Jesus' authority!

Can you imagine what "flashback" goes through the devil's mind when he comes face to face with some fellow wearing God's armor and God's helmet with God's weapons in each hand? As long as that fellow only speaks God's Words, the enemy will think, "that must be God inside there!" Do not neglect any of the armor you have been given. Wear it all. Keep the devil on the defensive and occupy until Jesus comes!

Impacting My World Confession

I take on the helmet of salvation and lay hold on the sword of the Spirit, which is able to build me up and keep me up in battle. I can root out, pull down, and destroy all the works of darkness. In Jesus' Name I Declare It! Amen!

What is the Spirit saying to me?

_____
_____
_____
_____
_____
_____
_____
_____
_____

He who has an ear, let him hear what the Spirit says...
(Revelation 2:11)

Confession 40

THE WORLD IS WAITING FOR YOU

For the earnest expectation of the creation eagerly waits for the revealing of the sons of God.
(Romans 8:19)

Daily Word Weapon: Psalm 139:13-18; John 14:12; Ephesians 3:20

You are the solution to a problem on earth. By being an answer to the problems on earth, you not only make the world a better place, but you also make your presence irreplaceable! Jesus is the answer to every problem in the world today. Without Him there is no other way out, because He is the way. Therefore, If you have received Christ into your heart, then you are in Christ and Christ is in you. Therefore, think of this phenomenon, part of the solution to the world's predicament is in your hands.

Many want to do great things for God but they do not take time to activate His nature in them. We humans tend to have the nature of what or who we closely associate with. To greatly impact our world by walking in a high level of supernatural grace and power, we need to know God intimately. This requires that we seek Him unreservedly. Seeking God may not come that easy because there are many things competing for our attention. To *really* seek Him, despite many distractions, we have to desire Him more than anything!

Do you love Him? If you love Him, you will take delight in His Word, and meditate on it day and night. As you do that, your eyes will be enlightened to know about your earthly assignment, and in so doing, you impact your world the more. God has prepared glorious things for those who love Him. Make a decision today to find and fulfill your divine purpose, because the world needs what you have. *Discover* your unique gifts. *Develop* them enough to deploy them properly and be a blessing to your world. The whole world is waiting *expectantly* for your manifestation! Your future is *pregnant* with *possibility!*

Impacting My World Confession

I am fearfully and wonderfully made. I am God's workmanship, created in Christ Jesus for good works. I will be a good steward of the manifold grace, gifts and abilities of God upon my life. I will minister with the authority which God gives to me to impact my world for Jesus Christ, and prepare the world for His return. In Jesus' Name I Declare It! Amen!

What is the Spirit saying to me?

_____
_____
_____
_____
_____
_____
_____
_____
_____

He who has an ear, let him hear what the Spirit says...
(Revelation 2:11)

MEDITATIVE PRAYER

Lord, it is my desire to know You more and I declare that, by the redemptive power of the blood of Jesus, I purge myself of anything that can prevent me from getting more intimate with You. I am thirsting for You, fill me to overflow, so that out of my belly shall flow rivers of living water. My desire is to continually be in communion with You. To behold Your beautiful Presence and to receive revelation for my destiny.

Father God, I am tired of toiling and doing everything my own way. I surrender to You. Give rest to my soul, for You are gentle and lowly in heart. I have resolved to focus on Your Word and let Your peace, which surpasses all understanding, guard my heart and mind through Christ Jesus. It is my longing to always be Your friend. For that reason, give me the grace to constantly meditate on Your Word and obey Your commandments.

My fruitfulness depends on me abiding in Your Word and living by it. Let Your Word which is full of life and spirit, pierce my soul and spirit and purge every impurity out of me, so that my life can continually radiate Your glory. I purpose to be Your disciple until I meet You in glory. I want to love as You do. Let Your Word dwell richly in me, and grant me, according to the riches of Your glory, to be strengthened with might through Your Spirit in my inner man.

This is the only way that I can be rooted and grounded in love. Help me to know the love of Your Son which is beyond knowledge. I want to always be ready to tell everyone of the reason that I have such hope in me. My ultimate yearning is to be like You, Jesus, in everything I do, whether openly or in secret. Therefore, take me deeper in Your Word and help me to know the breadth, and length, and depth, and height of Your Word, so that I can be filled with all the fullness of You, Father.

As I daily look into Your Word, Lord, let the Spirit of Your Word transform me into Your image from glory to glory. Anoint me specially to be Your duplicate, representing You in the earth realm and helping others to be reconciled to You. The whole world is slowly sinking into chaos, strengthen and help me to be a good steward of Your manifold grace upon my life, so that I can minister with the divine ability You conferred on me.

Father! This is of the utmost importance to me, because it is my delight to impact the world for Jesus Christ and make a lasting impact on my generation and generations to come. In Jesus mighty name, Amen!

SCRIPTURE REFERENCES FOR THE MEDITATION

THIRSTING FOR GOD	DIVINE REST
Psalm 42:1-3	Isaiah 26:3
Isaiah 55:1-3	Matthew 11:28-29
Matthew 5:6	Philippians 4:6-7

ABIDING IN THE WORD & FRUITFULNESS	GOD KIND OF LOVE
John 15:4-14	I John 4:8
Matthew 13:22-23	I John 4:16-18
Hebrews 4:12-13	John 13:34-35

CHRISTLIKENESS	GODLY LEGACY
Ephesians 3:16-19	II Corinthians 5:18-19
Colossians 3:16	John 14:12
I Peter 3:15	I Peter 4:10-11
	Acts 13:36a

PRAYER TO RECEIVE SALVATION

In order to start a productive relationship with God, you must surrender your life to the Lordship of Jesus Christ. If you have not accepted Jesus Christ as your Lord and Savior, I encourage you to pray the following prayer aloud in order to receive your salvation.

Dear God, I come to you believing that Jesus died on the cross and was raised from the dead to save my soul. I ask you to come into my heart and change me from within enabling me to enter into Your way of living. I confess with my mouth that I believe Jesus died for me and I now receive your gift of salvation. I am now born again. I confess that Jesus Christ is the Son of God and He is now the Lord of my life. Amen.

This is the wisest decision you have ever made. Please, do not look back. Endeavor to find a Bible-believing ministry where the unadulterated Word of God is being preached and taught. Begin to worship there regularly and attend Bible study. Be sure to read, study your bible and pray daily. Always ask the Holy Spirit to teach you His word before you study.

Welcome to the kingdom of light. May the Lord God bless and uphold you, in Jesus' Mighty Name! I am waiting to hear from you. You can contact me through my address toward the end of the book or my website.

ABOUT THE AUTHOR

J.E Bamidele Sturdivant, Sr. is the pastor of Faith United Ministries and is known worldwide as a blessing to the body of Christ. His unique style of simply, yet powerfully conveying Biblical principles has drawn millions to the cross and set the stage for massive deliverances and healings in the lives of God's people.

A native Washingtonian, J.E Sturdivant has made a divine connection to Nigeria through his God-appointed relationship with his Father in the Lord, E.A Adeboye. Heralded by Newsweek as one of the 50 Most Powerful world leaders, Adeboye has fully received J.E Sturdivant as a special son and poured mightily into his life in immeasurable ways. Adeboye, with the care of a father, named J.E Sturdivant "Bamidele," which is translated to mean *follow me home*.

Their relationship mirrors that of the prophet Elijah and his protégé, Elisha. As with these Biblical men of God, Bamidele has seen the ascension of Adeboye to greater heights in the Lord. In turn, the same mantle has fallen on him. Since their divine connection, Bamidele's ministry has been marked by the miraculous. Countless testimonies of actual resurrections from the dead, healing from cancer and astounding breakthroughs on every level speak to the authenticity of God's hand on his life and ministry.

A master teacher, Bamidele diligently studies to show himself worthy unto God and in the process earned degrees in Ministry. In turn, the sound Biblical truths he shares undoubtedly remind the world that holiness and excellence are the true hallmark of every Christ-follower.

An accomplished author, Bamidele has written *No Longer Crippled...From Trauma To Triumph!*, which outlines the blueprint for a wholistically, successful life. He also authored sections of *From One Brother To Another*, an inspirational devotional for men of all ethnicities, ages, and social backgrounds.

His most recent releases, *A Divine Hunger*, is a forty day devotional which challenges every believer to live a life of holiness supported by an appetite for the Master's Presence. While, *Learning To Soar* is a step-by-step manual that goes to the root of one's adversities and teaches them how to rise above them victoriously.

He was selected as the Guest Chaplain to offer prayer in the United States Senate in the presence of President Barack Obama, who was serving as United States Senator from Illinois at the time. His anointed and dynamic preaching style has also garnered the attention of other political officials.

He is a greatly esteemed and sought after teacher and evangelist who frequently ministers extensively throughout North America, the Caribbean, Africa, Asia, and Europe. J.E. Bamidele and his wife, Pamela D. have been married for over 33 years, and are the proud parents of four adult children.

You can contact J.E Bamidele Sturdivant using the mediums listed below. Although he cannot respond personally to all correspondences, he would love to get your feedback.

J.E.S. Ministries
7905 Fernham Lane,
District Heights
Maryland 20747
USA

Phone: 301-736-2383
Email: pastor@jesturdivantministries.org
Website: www.jesturdivantministries.org

Please include your testimony of help received from this book when you write. Your prayer requests are welcome.

You can order additional copies of this book @ **www.jesturdivantministries.org** or by mail through the postal address above.

OTHER BOOKS BY THE MINISTRY

No Longer Crippled

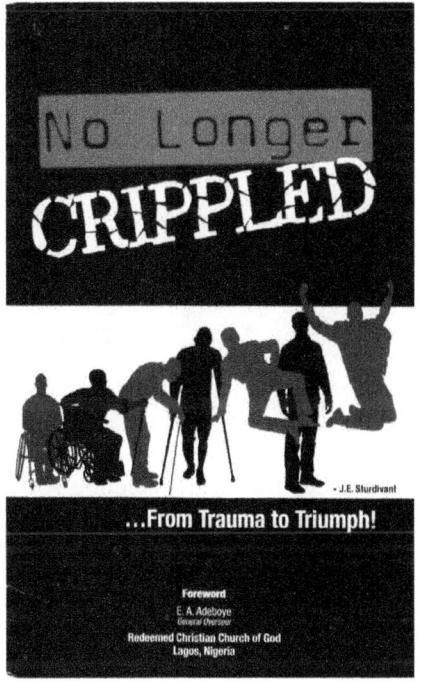

Adversity. It's one of the guarantees that come with being human. We experience it. We expect it. But it's how we choose to deal with it that shapes our lives, both negatively and positively. Adversity can leave us crippled in our emotions, our relationships, and our finances. However, God, in all His grace, equips us with the prescription and therapy to heal us in those hurting areas. In this book, J.E Sturdivant shows us that with God working and moving in our lives, we can triumph and use adversity to our advantage.

A Divine Hunger

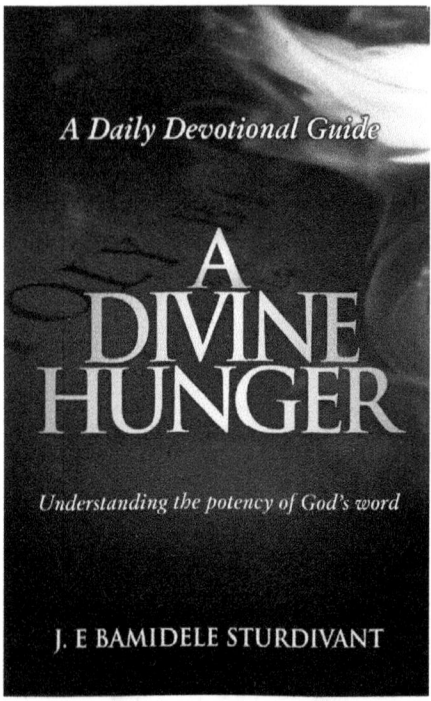

A Divine Hunger is a piece that will challenge you to grow in your walk with God. It is full of revelation knowledge from God's word on how to develop a hunger and a heart for the word, keep your mind on the word, live by the word and be liberated by the word. Many run helter skelter looking for solutions to their personal problems but the most enduring way to be secured in life is to develop an intimate relationship with God through His word.

Our lives glorify God when we bear fruit as we abide in Him and His words remain in us. This is only possible when we unreservedly commit to Him and value the relationship with Him above anything else in the world. No matter how gloomy your circumstances may be, this book will energize you and help you to experience the abundant life in all your endeavors. Be blessed as you read.

Learning To Soar

God's desire for us is to rise from glory to glory. As such, He has made provision for us to attain the greatest heights in life. However, negligence and slothfulness can open the door for demonic activity that brings about hindrances in our lives. These events can ultimately cause a delay in the fulfillment of God's plan for us. *Learning To Soar* takes you to the root cause of these dilemmas, showing you the *'success-proof'* tactics for rising above your adversary *and* to keep soaring.

With a unique blend of biblical knowledge and spiritual insight, this book brings to light the strategies the enemy uses to launch his attacks. Discover what you need to know to stand strong against the enemy and put him under your feet. The insights found in this book, if practiced, will help you to alter your present situation, as well as prepare and position you for a glorious future.

WATCH OUT! THE FOLLOWING BOOKS ARE TO BE RELEASED SHORTLY BY THE MINISTRY

1. HEARING AND KNOWING GOD'S VOICE

2. WHAT DOES THE FLESH HAS TO SAY?

3. MORE THAN A CONQUEROR
   (*Winning Spiritual Warfare*)

4. RECOGNIZING WHEN THE DEVIL SPEAKS
   (*Silencing the voice of the enemy*)

5. PEACE